Looking at Egyptian Myths and Legends

Isis

and

Osiris

Geraldine Harris

NTC Publishing Group
Lincolnwood, Illinois USA

Published by NTC Publishing Group
4255 West Touhy Avenue
Lincolnwood (Chicago), Illinois 60646-1775, USA

First published in the United Kingdom in 1996 by British
Museum Press

**Library of Congress Cataloging-in-Publication Data
is available from the Library of Congress**

Designed by Carla Turchini
Printed in Slovenia

Front cover: Winged goddess painted inside the coffin of
Djedhoriufankh, a priest from Thebes *c.* 1050 BC.

GERALDINE HARRIS lectures in Egyptology at
Cambridge University, England, and has written
numerous books for children and adults.

Contents

People in the Story

Taous and Thaues	Twin sisters living near Memphis (Egypt)
Khonouphis	A priest in the temple of Ptah
Ptolemy	The king of Egypt, ruling with his brother and sister

The Gods and Goddesses

Anubis	Jackal god, who looks after tombs and mummies
Geb	Earth god
Hathor	Goddess of love and motherhood
Horus	Hawk god, the son of Isis and Osiris
Isis	Great goddess of magic, sister and wife of Osiris
Khephri	Beetle god of dawn
Nephthys	Sister of Isis
Nout	Sky goddess
Osiris	Husband of Isis, later the king of the dead
Ptah	God of crafts, chief god of Memphis
Ra-Atum	Creator of the world, the sun god
Sekhmet	Lioness goddess of death and destruction
Selqet	Scorpion goddess
Seth	Jealous brother of Osiris, the enemy of Horus
Shu	God of the air, first son of Ra-Atum
Tefenet	First daughter of Ra-Atum, mother of Nout and Geb
Thoth	Lord of the moon, god of wisdom

Isis and Osiris

The goddess Isis and her brother Osiris were worshipped by the ancient Egyptians. Most of ancient Egypt was empty desert. It was hot by day and cold by night. Rain was almost unheard of. The great river Nile flowed through a valley in the center of Egypt. It split into several rivers in the marshlands of the north. Once a year, the Nile flooded its valley and water and rich mud were spread across the land. Then the Egyptians could grow enough food for everyone. The chief city of ancient Egypt was Memphis.

More than two thousand years ago, two young sisters lived in Memphis. They were twins and their names were Taous and Thaues. Their father was dead. Their mother was living with a soldier. She was unkind to the girls. Taous and Thaues had been left some money by their father but their mother gave it to the twins' half-brother instead.

Like other poor people, Taous and Thaues were forced to go and live in the City of the Dead, on the west bank of the Nile. All along the edge of the desert was a huge graveyard that had been used for thousands of years. Kings and queens, priests and nobles, and all kinds of sacred animals were buried there. The graveyard was crowded with pyramids and tombs and temples. Taous and Thaues took refuge in one of the temples at a place now called Saqqara.

Sometimes they earned a little money at funerals. When a rich person died, women and children were paid to follow the coffin weeping and wailing. Thaues could always make herself cry by pretending that the dead person was her father. Taous had to hold a cut onion to her face to make the tears come.

A bronze figure of an Apis Bull. The ancient Egyptians believed that part of the spirit of a god could live on earth in the body of a special animal. These animals acted as messengers between people and the gods. The Apis Bull was the most important sacred animal in Egypt. He was linked with two gods, Ptah and Osiris.

An Apis Bull had to be black and white. Priests searched Egypt for a calf with the right markings. The finding of a new Apis Bull was celebrated with a great public holiday. The calf and its mother were taken to the temple of Ptah at Memphis. The home of the Apis Bull was like a small palace.

When the bull died, he was buried as splendidly as a king.

37448

Mostly the twins lived by begging. They often went hungry.

One day a visitor asked to see the twins. They could tell from his shaven head and the special white clothes that he wore, that he was a priest.

"My name is Khonouphis," he told them. "I am a priest in the temple of Ptah."

He asked the girls how old they were and whether they could sing. The twins were very puzzled by his questions.

"I am here," said Khonouphis, "because the Apis Bull is dead."

The twins knew that a great black and white bull was always kept in one of the temples and treated like a god. The tombs of the Apis Bulls of earlier times were close to where they lived.

"When an Apis Bull dies," explained Khonouphis, "we bury him as if he was the god Osiris himself. The whole city comes to the funeral and the stories of the gods are acted out. King Ptolemy has ordered me to search for a pair of sisters to play the twin goddesses, Isis and Nephthys. I think that you are just the girls I'm looking for."

Thaues asked what they would have to do. Taous asked whether they would be paid.

"You would have to weep and wail, as you've done at other funerals. You would also sing songs for the dead god. If you'll come and stay with my family in Memphis, I will teach you the words of the songs and everything else you need to know. After the funeral you will share in a great feast and you will be paid in silver."

The twins agreed to go. Khonouphis took them down into the Nile valley. They came to the high mudbrick walls of the temple of Ptah, the chief god of Memphis. The twins were amazed by the huge stone buildings inside the walls. They saw bright flags flying from tall cedar poles, obelisks tipped with gold, and many stone statues of kings and gods.

The Creation

The twins had been taught to say their prayers, but they didn't know much about the gods. "I will tell you the story of our gods from the beginning," said Khonouphis.

He took the twins across the temple courtyard to a great slab of black stone.

This stone slab once stood in the temple of Ptah at Memphis. It is called the "Shabaqo Stone," after the king who had it made. King Shabaqo visited the temple around 700 BC.

In Egypt, books were written on long scrolls made of papyrus or leather. Shabaqo found that one of the oldest scrolls in the temple library had been damaged by insects. He had the scroll copied onto this slab, to make sure that the priests of the temple would always be able to read it.

The writing on the stone is in the hieroglyphic script. It tells how Ptah created the world and how the god Horus came to be ruler of Egypt. Some people think this is one of the earliest accounts of the creation of the world to survive.

Years later when people no longer worshipped at the temple, local farmers used the slab as a mill-stone for grinding corn. You can see how damaged it is.

"Centuries ago, King Shabaqo found that one of the ancient scrolls in our temple library was being eaten by bookworms. He had the words from the scroll carved on this hard piece of stone, so that they will last forever. The stone tells us how our world began, back in the First Time. Let your ears hear and your hearts understand."

Before the beginning of time, there was nothing but the ocean of chaos. There was no light. There was no land. The dark ocean went on forever. Then the first being, the Creator, woke up in the black waters. The Creator has many names. Here in Memphis we call him Ptah. In Heliopolis, the oldest of cities, he is called Ra-Atum.

The first mound of land appeared in the ocean of chaos. The Creator, Ra-Atum, now had a place to be. He realized that he was lonely. In his heart Ra-Atum thought about a son and a daughter. His thoughts turned into words. His words turned into a god and a goddess. He sneezed out Shu. He spat out Tefenet. Shu and Tefenet brought life and truth into the world. The First Time had begun.

The only light came from the fiery eyes of Ra-Atum. Shu and Tefenet tried to leave the mound and were swept away by the stormy ocean. Ra-Atum was lonely again without his children. He pulled one of his own eyes out of his head. The eye turned into a fiery goddess. Ra-Atum sent the Eye goddess out into the darkness to look for Shu and Tefenet.

She found the lost children and she brought them back. Ra-Atum cried tears of joy when he hugged his children again. The Eye goddess was jealous when she saw that Ra-Atum had already grown another eye. She cried tears of anger. Ra-Atum turned her into a cobra and let her coil around his brow. She defended him by spitting poison at his enemies.

Ra-Atum made a world in the middle of the great ocean. He was the light of the sun. His power brought everything to life. Out of the depths of the ocean came huge snakes. These were the chaos serpents. They hated everything that Ra-Atum had made. The most dangerous of them is the great monster, Apep. He is big enough to swallow the sun. The gods will fight him until the world ends.

"But where did people come from?" asked Taous.

"The first people were made out of the tears of the Creator," answered Khonouphis. "Some say that we come from the tears that Ra-Atum cried when the Eye brought back Shu and Tefenet. Others say that we come from the tears that the Eye goddess cried when she saw the new eye in Ra-Atum's head. Tears of joy or tears of anger, we are all the children of Ra-Atum."

The Children of the Sky

Thaues had a question.

"What about Isis and Nephthys? How were they born?"

"The gods are not like us," answered Khonouphis "They don't have to follow the rules made for people. Among the gods it was right for a brother and sister to marry. Our king, Ptolemy, is like a god on Earth. So it is right for him to marry his sister, queen Cleopatra. He is doing what was done in the First Time. This is what happened."

Back in the First Time, the god Shu married his sister Tefenet and they had two children called Geb and Nout. Geb is our father the earth who lies under us. Nout is our mother the sky who arches above us. Geb and Nout loved each other so much, they couldn't bear to be apart for a moment. They held each other so tightly, there was no space for anything between them. Nothing could grow out of the earth. Nothing could live under the sky. There wasn't even room for the children of Geb and Nout to be born.

Ra-Atum sent for Shu, the god of the shining air. He told Shu to part Geb and Nout. Shu forced them to let go of each other. He pushed them apart. Shu grew to gigantic size. He lifted Nout on his hands and held her high above Geb. The breath of Shu filled the space between with air. So now the sky can only touch the earth at the far horizon. Geb and Nout can never be together again until the end of the world.

The drawing on this papyrus shows the air god Shu holding apart his two children, Nout the sky goddess and Geb the earth god. Two ram-headed spirits are helping Shu to hold up the sky.

In Egyptian art, the sky can also be shown as a giant cow with stars along her belly. The feet of the cow touch the four corners of the earth. The Egyptians may have thought of the earth as a flat rectangle surrounded by water. Some writings describe huge caverns under the earth which the sun had to pass through every night.

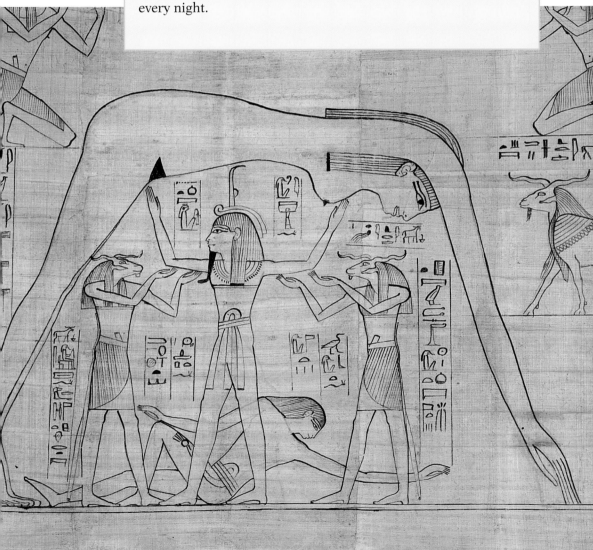

After the sky and the earth were separated, Nout gave birth to five children in five days. The oldest child was Osiris, who was born wearing a crown. The oldest daughter was Isis. She fell in love with Osiris when they were still inside their mother. Next came a son, who turned into a falcon and flew up into the sky. Then there was a daughter, Nephthys. She and Isis were loving sisters. Last came another son, Seth. Right from the start, Seth hated his oldest brother because Osiris was going to be king. It was an evil day when Seth was born. Even now, the birthday of Seth is the unluckiest day of the year.

"We must have been born on an unlucky day," said Taous. "We have a brother who hates us too."

Khonouphis nodded.

"If you were born on one of the unlucky days of the year, bad things may happen, but don't despair. The gods can help us change our fate."

The Secret Name

As they walked across the huge temple courtyard, Khonouphis pointed to a mudbrick building.

"That is the House of Life, where we keep calendars of lucky and unlucky days and many other book-scrolls. I can't take you inside, because secret books of magic are stored there. Only the priests of the House of Life are allowed to read them. We use the spells to protect our temple and our king and anyone who asks for our help. Among the gods, Thoth and Isis are the great magicians. One of our books tells how Isis won the strongest magic of all."

Ra-Atum had made himself out of nothing. He made heaven and earth, water and air. He made hundreds of gods and goddesses. He made men and animals, reptiles and fishes and birds. He ruled over heaven and earth and all the gods called him father. Egypt was Ra-Atum's favorite country. He had a great palace there. Every day, Ra-Atum traveled through the Nile valley and the deserts and marshlands of Egypt.

The children of the sky goddess grew up. Osiris was handsome and kind. Isis was beautiful and clever. Osiris and Isis loved each other. They became husband and wife. The gods can change their shapes whenever they want, but all the shapes of Seth were ugly. He was a monster. Seth wanted Nephthys as his wife but she hated him. She chose to live with Isis and Osiris instead.

Of all the family of gods, Isis was the cleverest. She was more cunning than millions of gods and spirits. She had learned all the strongest spells. She knew about everything in heaven and earth. The only thing that Isis didn't know was the secret name of Ra-Atum. It was the power in his secret name that Ra-Atum used to make life. In her heart, Isis longed for the power of the secret name. She wanted it for the children she planned to have with Osiris. Isis had to be sure that Ra-Atum would choose her son to rule Egypt.

To work magic against Ra-Atum, Isis needed something that had come from his body. She watched and waited until she saw a drop of spit fall from Ra-Atum's mouth. Isis mixed the spit with a ball of earth. She kneaded the earth until it was soft, and shaped it into a snake. The spit of Ra-Atum and the magic of Isis brought the snake to life. She hid it at a cross-roads where Ra-Atum walked every day.

The next morning Ra-Atum left his palace to look at everything he had made. He was followed by many gods and goddesses. He traveled through the desert and along the banks of the river Nile. He came to the place where Isis had hidden the snake. Ra-Atum felt a sudden, burning pain. It spread as fast as fire in a pine wood. The snake had bitten him, but no one saw it creep away.

Ra-Atum screamed with pain. All the gods and goddesses crowded around him. They asked what the trouble was. At first Ra-Atum could not answer. He shook all over as the snake's venom spread through his body. At last, Ra-Atum found the strength to call out,

"Come to me, all my children. Something has hurt me, but I don't know what. I didn't see it happen. It can't be anything that I have made. No one knows my secret name, so no one can put a spell on me. Fetch all my children here. Fetch me the wise gods and goddesses who know the strongest magic."

All the children, and the grandchildren, and the great-grandchildren of Ra-Atum came hurrying. They wailed at the sight of him and tore their hair. No one seemed to know what to do, except Isis.

"What has happened, father of the gods?" asked Isis. "Perhaps a snake has bitten you? I will fight the poison with my sorcery."

Ra-Atum answered,

"Some unknown force has poisoned me. It isn't fire and it isn't water, but I feel hotter than flames and colder than ice. I'm soaked in sweat. I can't stop trembling and my eyes can hardly see."

Crafty Isis said,

"Tell me your true name, divine father. Then I can help you with my spells."

"I am the one who made heaven and earth," Ra-Atum

told her. "I shaped the mountains and the seas. I made the bull for the cow and a mate for every creature. When I open my eyes, there is light. When I close my eyes, there is darkness. I created day and night and the seasons of the year. I make the river Nile flood every year so that the land can grow crops. I gave fire so that people can have food and warmth and light. My name is Khepri in the morning, Ra at noon, and Atum at night.'

Isis shook her head.

"None of those names is your true name. You must tell me the secret, or I cannot drive away the poison."

The pain became worse. Ra-Atum couldn't bear it any longer.

The blue beetle Khephri is one of the many forms of the sun god. Isis and Nephthys are shown adoring Khephri on this colourful glazed pendant. It was made for a woman called Henutemheb who lived in Memphis over three thousand years ago.

You can tell the twin goddesses apart by their headdresses. Isis (on the left) has a miniature throne on her head. Nephthys wears the signs that write her name.

You can also see two amulets (lucky charms) linked with the story of Osiris and Isis: the djed pillar (left) and the tyet knot (right). The tyet knot is sometimes called the 'Isis knot'.

"Come close, daughter Isis. I will whisper the name in your ear. It will pass from my heart to yours. Promise never to tell it to anyone, except to your son." Isis promised and Ra-Atum whispered his secret name to her.

Then Isis began her spell. She used all her powers to drive out the poison.

"Out fiery poison," she said. "Leave Ra-Atum, leave the god. I have power over you because I made you. I have power over you because I know your true name."

The snake had been made from the spit of Ra-Atum, so its true name was the name of the god. Isis spoke the secret name and the poison was forced to leave the body of Ra-Atum. He was healed. Isis was overjoyed. Her plan had worked. She could pass on the power of the secret name to her son.

Khonouphis started to walk away.

"But what was the secret name?" asked Thaues.

"Ah," said Khonouphis, "That must never be written down or said aloud. The greatest magicians know it, but they only whisper it to their sons or daughters."

Taous was puzzled.

"If Ra-Atum is the greatest god, why didn't he guess what Isis had done?"

"We mustn't question the actions of a god, little one. Perhaps he knew that Isis would need the power of his name one day."

The Anger of Ra-Atum

Khonouphis made the twins stand back to look at the scenes
carved high on the front of the temple. They showed a great
battle. A king of Egypt was driving across the battlefield in a
chariot, shooting arrows at foreign enemies. "In this age,
people are always fighting wars. Back in the First Time, it was
different. Humankind could have lived in peace for ever, if only
we'd obeyed the Creator."

Ra-Atum ruled the whole world but he had grown old. His
bones were like silver. His skin was like gold. His hair was
like lapis-lazuli. The men and women who lived on earth forgot
that Ra-Atum had made the world. They got tired of following
his orders. People started to plot against Ra-Atum.

He soon knew about their plans. Ra-Atum ordered the gods
to come to a secret meeting. Osiris and Isis and all the other
gods gathered at the palace.

Ra-Atum said to them, "The creatures who came from my
tears are plotting to kill me. Shall I destroy them all? Or shall I
forgive them?"

None of the gods spoke up for humanity. One of them said,
"Send your Eye to catch and kill the ungrateful creatures."

The Eye goddess was the cobra who coiled around the head
of Ra-Atum. She defended him against his enemies with fire
and poison. She could take on many shapes.

Ra-Atum sent her out in the form of a lioness. In a single
day she killed half of all the people who lived on earth. She tore
them apart and drank their blood. This was how death first
came into the world. When the Eye goddess returned to the
palace, Ra-Atum gave her a new name, Sekhmet. That means
"The Powerful One."

Ra-Atum knew that humankind would not dare to rebel
against him again. He felt sorry for the people who were left,
but once Sekhmet had tasted blood not even the King of Gods
could make her stop killing. Ra-Atum had to find a way to trick
her.

The shadows cast by the sun were Ra-Atum's messengers on
Earth. He sent the shadows to the far south of Egypt to fetch

some red stone. In Heliopolis, people had built the first temple to worship Ra-Atum. The high priest of this temple was a good man. Ra-Atum told the high priest how to fool Sekhmet. First, the women of the temple worked all night to brew seven thousand jars of beer. Then the high priest had the red stone ground to a powder. He put the powder into the jars. The beer all turned the colour of blood. While it was still dark, Ra-Atum went to the temple of Heliopolis. He inspected the beer. He ordered all seven thousand jars to be poured out on the ground.

At dawn, Sekhmet came back to kill the rest of the people of Earth. She saw what looked like a lake of blood. Sekhmet admired her own reflection in the lake. She began to lap up the beer, thinking that it was blood. She drank all seven thousand jars. Sekhmet got so drunk she couldn't remember what people looked like. She forgot all about killing humanity and went back to the palace of Ra-Atum.

Once a year we remember how Ra-Atum saved us from Sekhmet. There is a big feast and everyone drinks too much beer.

Khonouphis pointed to a statue of a woman with the head of a lioness.

"That is Sekhmet. We worship her here as the wife of the god Ptah."

Thaues shuddered.

"She looks so fierce."

"You are right to be frightened, little one. When the gods are angry, they still send Sekhmet to punish us. Now she comes as plague and fever in the hottest days of the year."

"Why are the gods so cruel?" asked Taous.

"The gods have given us the knowledge to defend ourselves," said Khonouphis. "The priests of Sekhmet study medicine in the House of Life. They help sick people all over the city."

The terrifying lioness goddess Sekhmet was worshipped in Memphis. This painting of Sekhmet and other gods comes from one of the longest papyrus rolls ever found. It is 45 yards long! The papyrus lists the gifts made to temples by King Ramses III.

Sekhmet could take on the form of a lioness or a cobra to attack the enemies of the sun god. Both forms are combined with her human shape in this picture. In front of her is her husband, the god Ptah. Behind her is their son Nefertem. The figure on the right is King Ramses himself.

Ra-Atum leaves Egypt

Khonouphis took the twins to an area of the courtyard where visitors were allowed to leave gifts for the gods. Men and women were offering precious scented oils and jars of the best wine. The poorest people could only afford to bring a cup of water and a loaf of bread. Set into a mudbrick wall were stone and wooden plaques left by centuries of visitors. The twins couldn't help smiling when they saw that some of the plaques were carved with dozens of ears.

"A good heart is the best gift to bring," said Khonouphis. "Those ears are to show that the god listens to everyone who prays to him. The Creator still loves us, even though we drove him away from earth."

After the people of earth rebelled against him, Ra-Atum felt sick at heart. He was tired of ruling. All he wanted to do was sink back into the ocean of chaos. The family of gods begged him not to be sad. The good people on Earth promised to obey Ra-Atum and to fight his enemies. Even so, Ra-Atum did not want to live among humans anymore.

The goddess Nout turned herself into a cow. Ra-Atum climbed on her back and she carried the weary god up into the heavens. Then Ra-Atum made the fields of paradise, so that the souls of the dead could live near him.

The sky had never been so far above the earth before. Nout began to shake with fear. Ra-Atum summoned the giant Shu and the eight gods of Twilight to hold her up. Ra-Atum made the stars and the moon so that people need not be afraid of the night. The wise god Thoth was lord of the moon. He carried out all Ra-Atum's orders.

Ra-Atum spoke to the earth god, Geb. He told him to beware of the chaos snakes that lived inside the earth. Now that Ra-Atum was no longer living on earth, the forces of chaos would try to destroy life. Ra-Atum gave Osiris the job of protecting the world and its people. So Osiris was crowned king of Egypt and of all the other countries. Isis became queen. Osiris sat on the throne and all the gods of Egypt bowed down to him.

Every day, Ra-Atum traveled across the sky in a great boat.

Each sunset, the sun boat entered the underworld. The terrible demons of chaos hid in the dark caves of the underworld. Each night Ra-Atum faced many dangers. The magic of Isis and the strength of Seth were needed to defend the sun boat in the darkest hour of the night. Each dawn the sun boat escaped from the underworld to bring new life to Egypt.

Khonouphis looked up at the sky.

"The priests who serve in the temple get up before dawn. They use strong magic against the demons of darkness. The priests greet the sun when it rises and give thanks for each new day. We all have to help in the fight against chaos."

This picture shows Ra-Atum sitting in the sun boat, with the golden disc of the sun around him. He is wearing the double crown of an Egyptian king.

Egyptians thought the sun journeyed across the sky in a boat and entered the underworld each evening. This sun boat looks like the simple boats made from papyrus stems that the Egyptians used on the Nile from very early times.

The picture comes from a "Book of the Dead" made for the scribe Ani. The spells in this book were supposed to help the dead survive the dangers of the afterlife. Ani's papyrus is famous for its beautiful paintings. You can see other pictures from Books of the Dead on pages 41 and 42-43.

The Murder of Osiris

More and more people were entering the temple courtyard.

"We must go where no one can overhear us," said Khonouphis. "What I have to tell you now isn't for everyone's ears."

He led them outside the temple walls towards a tent beside a lake. As they came closer, the twins noticed strange smells coming from the tent. Some were pleasant, some were not.

"This is where the body of the Apis bull is being prepared for mummification," said Khonouphis. "No one wants to see the embalmers at their gruesome work. We won't be disturbed here. Come close and listen."

Ra-Atum reigned in the heavens and Osiris on earth. Isis stood behind the throne of Osiris, to protect him with her magic.

A stone statue of Isis and Osiris. Isis is carved larger than her husband because she is his protector.

Isis could appear as a beautiful woman or as a kite, a small bird of prey. The winged arms of the goddess suggest her bird form.

Osiris wears and holds symbols of Egyptian kingship. His crown is decorated with ostrich feathers and a uraeus (a royal cobra). He is holding a shepherd's crook (right) and a flail (left). The crook showed that the king would look after his people, like a good shepherd looks after his sheep. The flail was probably a kind of whip. It may have been a symbol of the power of the king to punish the wicked.

Osiris was a wise judge and a good king. He defended Egypt
from the enemies of life. He taught people how to farm the
land. He made the Nile flood and the crops grow. Everyone had
plenty to eat.

There was only one person who didn't love Osiris. Seth was
jealous of his brother. Thinking about Osiris made Seth so
angry it gave him nosebleeds. Seth believed that he should be
king, because he was the strongest of the children of Nout.
He was furious that both his sisters loved Osiris more than
they did him. In his heart, Seth plotted to kill Osiris and
become king.

Osiris often walked through Egypt to see that everything
was going well in his kingdom. Seth followed him. One day
he caught Osiris alone on the river bank. Seth spat fury at
his brother. The strong arm of Seth seized Osiris. Seth
struck down his brother.
Some say that Seth held Osiris under the Nile until he
drowned. Others say that Seth took the form of a wild bull
and trampled Osiris to death. Even that was not enough for
Seth. He tore the body of his brother apart and scattered the
pieces. Seth wanted to make sure that even the magic of Isis
could not bring Osiris back to life.

When Osiris didn't return to the palace, Isis knew that
something terrible had happened. She and her sister Nephthys
searched the deserts and the marshes and the river valley. On
the bank of the Nile, Isis found the head of Osiris. It took
twelve days to gather all the pieces of the body together.

Every creature must return to the Creator in the end, but Osiris
had died before his time. He and Isis still had no children.
There was no son to inherit his throne. In despair, Isis called
for the jackal god, Anubis, to help her. He is the deadly
guardian of all graveyards.

Anubis laid the mangled body of Osiris on a bed. Isis and Anubis worked together to make the body whole again. Then Anubis cut open the stomach of Osiris with a flint knife. He reached inside and drew out the soft organs. He put the lungs and the liver, the stomach and the intestines of Osiris into four jars. Anubis washed the body with wine and covered it with natron salts to preserve it.

After forty days the skin was dried out by the salt. Anubis washed away the salt with Nile water. He packed the stomach with frankincense and myrrh and sewed up the wound. Anubis wrapped the head and limbs and torso in fine linen bandages. He put amulets in the wrappings to protect the body. Anubis had turned Osiris into the first mummy.

A miniature pyramid from a tomb chapel, showing Anubis mummifying a body. At the top is Anubis in his fierce jackal form.

Below you can see the mummy on a couch and Anubis with a jackal's head. Under the couch are the four Canopic jars which hold the organs which Anubis has taken out of the mummy. The human-headed jar holds the liver, the baboon-headed jar has the lungs, the jackal-headed jar has the stomach, and the hawk-headed jar has the intestines.

Isis stands at the foot of the couch and Nephthys at the head. They are wringing their hands in mourning.

The body of Osiris would now keep for ever, but he was still dead. Isis knelt down at one end of the bed. Nephthys knelt down at the other. Isis shook loose her long hair and tore her clothes. She clawed up handfuls of dirt and threw them over her head. She called out to Osiris.

"I am your sister Isis, the one you loved. Come back to me, or I will flood Egypt with my tears. Come back to me!"

Nephthys said,

"Oh good king, come back to your body. Your two sisters are guarding you now. Open your eyes again, Osiris!"

Isis said,

"Let me see your face again. I am your sister, I am your wife. I am the queen of your heart. Come to this place in peace!"

All night long they mourned for Osiris. Over and over again, the sisters begged Osiris to come back to them. Isis turned herself into a bird. She hovered over Osiris. She fanned him with her wings to give him the breath of life. She used the power of the secret name of Ra.

The light of the sun brought Osiris to life again. His skin felt warm and his body began to move. Isis knew that it would only be for a brief while. She took Osiris in her arms for the last time. Then the soul of Osiris left his body.

As Khonouphis stopped speaking, a man came out of the embalming tent and knelt to wash his hands in the lake. He was wearing a jackal mask. The twins knew that he must be one of the Anubis men who dealt with corpses. They had seen the Anubis men at funerals, but the twins still found them frightening. Thaues asked if they could return to the temple.

The Punishment of Seth

As they walked back into the temple, Khonouphis pointed out a small stone building.

"The body of the Apis Bull will be soon taken into this embalming house. It is kept on a bed of alabaster until it's ready to be wrapped in linen. The priests will keep watch over it, just as Anubis guarded the body of Osiris from the hatred of Seth."

"I hope that Seth was horribly punished for what he did," said Taous.

"Listen, and you will hear how he was punished," answered Khonouphis.

Isis feared that Seth would again try to destroy the body of Osiris. Isis asked the wise god Thoth to say magic spells over the mummy. Thoth put a terrible curse on anyone who dared to touch the mummy of Osiris. The fierce god Anubis stood guard day and night.

A bronze amulet in the shape of the god Seth. An amulet is a small object, usually a piece of jewelry, thought to have magical powers. The owner of this amulet probably hoped that the legendary strength of Seth would protect him from his enemies.

Seth is shown with the body of a man and the head of a strange animal. The Seth animal has long ears, a curved snout, cloven hooves and a forked tail. People have guessed that this animal is based on a wild donkey, an aardvark, or even an okapi. It was probably meant to be a monster made up of several exotic animals.

Seth wears a crown. It is very rare for Seth to be shown as a king.

Seth did not dare to come near in his usual shape. He changed himself into a golden leopard. He planned to rip the body apart again. When Seth tried to reach the mummy, the invisible magic of Thoth grabbed him by the throat. While Seth was trapped by the curse, Anubis heated up a branding iron. Then he burned Seth with the branding iron over and over again. Since that day, all leopards have had spotted coats.

Next, Anubis took a sharp knife and skinned Seth. He hung the dripping skin on a pole to warn anyone else who might try to disturb the body of Osiris. Priests still wear leopard-skins in memory of the branding of Seth. We are all the guardians of Osiris.

Seth was in terrible pain, but even Anubis was not strong enough to kill him. Seth ran away and turned back into his usual monstrous shape. The people of Egypt, and most of the gods, were afraid of Seth. They had to obey him as if he was king.

In the meanwhile, the soul of Osiris had gone down into the underworld. He cried to Ra-Atum, "What is this terrible place? There is no air to breathe. There is nothing to eat or drink. It is darker than the darkest night. I am all alone. I have lost everyone I love."

The voice of Ra-Atum spoke to him.

"You no longer need air or food or water. Instead, you have eternal peace."

But Osiris wasn't comforted.

"I can't see your light. All the other gods can join you in the sun boat."

Then Ra-Atum told Osiris to be patient.

"Your fate is different from all the other gods. You are going to have a son. When your son Horus is old enough, he will be king. Horus will reign on earth. You will reign in the underworld. It will all happen as I have promised."

So the weary soul of Osiris waited in the darkness.

Thaues couldn't stop crying for Osiris. Taous wanted to know what happened to Isis.

"You will find out soon," promised Khonouphis, "but remember, the story of Osiris and Seth is a secret. You mustn't speak to anyone outside the temple about the murder of Osiris. Even talking about the evil of Seth in a careless way can give him power."

The twins promised to be careful.

Horus in the Marshes

Khonouphis brought the twins back to the the main entrance of the temple. He stopped beside a stone slab. It was covered with strange carvings of gods and monsters. A jar of water and a stone bowl stood in front of the slab. The back of the slab was covered in sacred writing. Khonouphis told the twins what the hieroglyphs said.

Seth took Isis prisoner. He locked her up and made her spin flax all day as if she was a slave. He took Nephthys back to his own house. Nephthys had to live with Seth as his wife. She hated him more than ever.

Isis found that she was pregnant. Most of the gods were too afraid of Seth to help her, but she still had some friends. The wise god Thoth came to her prison and helped her to escape by night. He told Isis that she must find a place to hide. He promised that Isis would have a son. When her son was grown up, the time would come for revenge.

The goddess Selqet sent seven scorpions to guard Isis on her journey. They kept their tails up, ready to sting anyone who threatened her. Isis and her scorpions travelled by day and hid by night. At last she reached the marshlands where the great Nile splits into three rivers. Near the town of Buto, she found a floating island. Papyrus plants and reeds grew on the island and it floated from place to place.

Hidden among the papyrus, Isis gave birth to a beautiful son. She called him Horus. The skin of baby Horus shone like

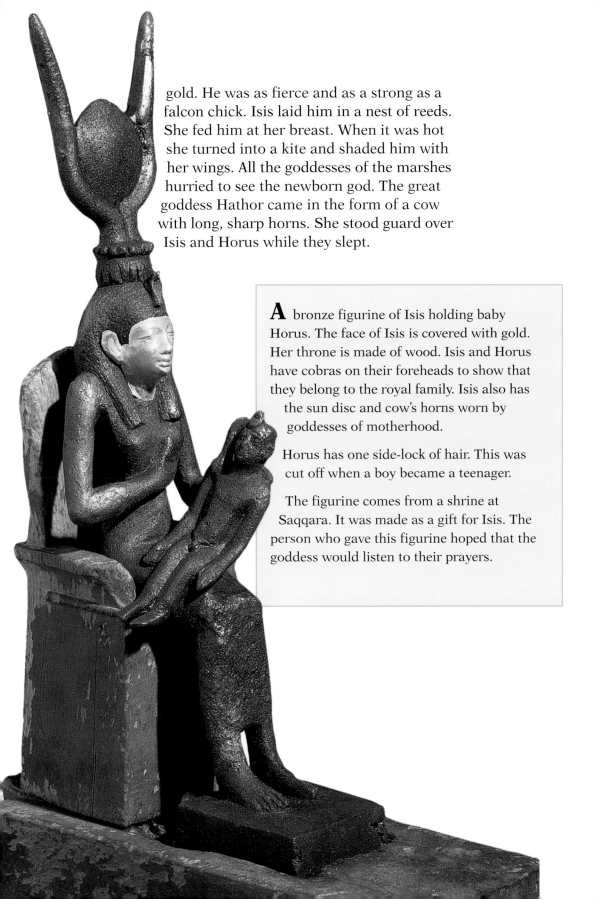

gold. He was as fierce and as a strong as a falcon chick. Isis laid him in a nest of reeds. She fed him at her breast. When it was hot she turned into a kite and shaded him with her wings. All the goddesses of the marshes hurried to see the newborn god. The great goddess Hathor came in the form of a cow with long, sharp horns. She stood guard over Isis and Horus while they slept.

A bronze figurine of Isis holding baby Horus. The face of Isis is covered with gold. Her throne is made of wood. Isis and Horus have cobras on their foreheads to show that they belong to the royal family. Isis also has the sun disc and cow's horns worn by goddesses of motherhood.

Horus has one side-lock of hair. This was cut off when a boy became a teenager.

The figurine comes from a shrine at Saqqara. It was made as a gift for Isis. The person who gave this figurine hoped that the goddess would listen to their prayers.

Isis could not stay with Horus all the time. When she was hungry she disguised herself as a poor peasant woman. She visited the marsh villages to beg for food. The wives of the fishermen who lived there were kind to her. While she was gone, the marsh goddesses watched over Horus and the floating island rocked like a cradle.

Whispers of a marvelous child born in the marshes reached Seth. He guessed this must be the son of Isis and Osiris. Seth wanted to kill his nephew while Horus was still young and weak. He couldn't get near the floating island because of the marsh goddesses. Seth was master of all the snakes that hid in the earth. He chose a snake that was small but very poisonous. He sent it to the marshes to kill Horus.

One day, Isis left the floating island to beg for food. Seth's snake crept through the marshes. No one saw it come. It found baby Horus fast asleep in his nest of reeds. The snake bit him on the foot. Horus woke up and began to cry. The snake slithered away. Horus screamed as the poison from the bite spread through his body.

When Isis came back from the village she saw at once that her baby was sick. Water dripped from his mouth and eyes. His skin was hot with fever. His pulse was very faint. She cradled him in her arms, but Horus was too weak to nurse. Isis was so frightened, she forgot all her magic. She began to cry because there was no one to help her. Her beloved Osiris was dead. Her brother Seth was her enemy. Her sister Nephthys was forced to live in his house.

The fishermen heard Isis crying and came to see what the matter was. They tried to comfort Isis, but they didn't know how to cure Horus. The fishermen sent for a wise woman who knew all about medicine. She came carrying an ankh – the sign of life. The wise woman guessed who Isis was. She said,

"Don't be afraid little Horus. Don't despair, Lady Isis. Your brother Seth can't enter this marsh. Death can't come to this holy place. Perhaps a scorpion or a snake has bitten your child."

Isis kneeled down and sniffed at Horus' breath. She smelled the poison inside him. Isis snatched up her baby. She danced around with him, like a live fish thrown on hot coals. She called out,

"Horus has been bitten! My lovely golden Horus has been poisoned!"

Horus wailed with pain.

The goddess Selqet hurried through the marshes to the island.

"Why are you crying Isis? What is the matter with Horus?"

"Horus has been bitten! My nestling, my innocent child, has been poisoned!" Then Selqet began to cry too. She said to Isis, "Call out to the sun god. Tell Ra-Atum what has happened."

The sun was just setting. Isis let out a great scream. At her scream, everything in the world stopped dead. The sun stood still in the sky. The winds that gave the breath of life to Egypt dropped away.

Ra-Atum didn't know why the sun boat could not move. He sent Thoth down to earth to find out who had screamed. When Thoth saw that it was Isis, he said,

"What is the matter, Isis? Surely, with all your magic powers nothing has happened to Horus. If you stop the sun boat there will be no tomorrow."

Isis was angry.

"There will be no tomorrow if my son dies. He is my only reason to live. Look, Horus has been poisoned! His uncle Seth must have done this wicked thing."

Thoth took baby Horus in his arms.

"Don't be afraid. Ra-Atum will not let you die, little Horus. You will get better and your mother will be happy again."

Then Thoth began to speak to the poison inside Horus.

"Horus is protected by Ra-Atum in the sky, by his mother Isis on earth, and by his father Osiris in the land of the dead. Get out poison! The magic of Thoth and the power of Ra-Atum will drive you out. Get out poison, or the sun boat cannot move. Get out poison, or the sun will never rise again. The world will stay dark and everything will die."

The poison came out of Horus like a little snake leaving his mouth. The pain and fever left with it.

"Horus is alive," said Thoth, "to be his mother's joy."

Thoth spoke to the goddesses of the marshes and the fishermen.

"Watch over this little one and his mother. One day he will be the ruler of Egypt."

He handed the baby god to Isis.

"I must go back to the sun boat, so the boat can sail on. Horus is alive. No poison can hurt him now." Thoth returned to the sky.

Horus was full of the magic of Thoth and the power of Ra-Atum. Seth sent other dangerous animals to try to kill Horus. The young god was too strong for them. Horus squeezed snakes and scorpions to death. He swung lions by the tail. He stamped on crocodiles. Just as he does in this carving.

The story of Isis in the marshes is written on the back of this stone stela (carved slab). Her son Horus is shown in the middle as a naked child fighting dangerous animals.

Because most ancient Egyptian children went barefoot, they were in danger of treading on scorpions or snakes.

The Egyptians used stelae like this one to treat stings and bites. They poured water over the magic words and carvings on the stela. The injured child had to drink the magic water. The hope was that the child would get better just as Horus did after he was poisoned.

Khonouphis picked up the jug. He poured water over the stone so that it trickled down into the bowl.

"Cup your hands and drink the water. As you swallow the water, you swallow the magic in the words. It will help you remember the story of Isis in the marshes and protect you against poison."

"I was stung by a little scorpion once," said Thaues. "It hurt for days."

She knelt down and scooped up some water. Taous drank some too. The magic water didn't taste any different from ordinary water.

Taous asked a question.

"Was Horus bitten to punish Isis for sending a snake to bite Ra-Atum?"

"Only the Creator knows," said Khonouphis. "Since that day, kind Isis cries for every sick child and Thoth uses his magic to heal them."

The Eye of Horus

"You have seen Horus as a human child," Khonouphis told the twins, "but Horus could also change himself into a fierce bird of prey. At some temples, tame hawks are kept to honor Horus."

"Did Horus fight Seth when he grew up?" asked Thaues.

"In many different ways," said Khonouphis. "This is what happened."

The years passed and Horus grew up into a handsome young god. Isis often told him the story of his father's murder. She warned Horus never to trust his uncle. Isis promised her son that he was born to be king of Egypt.

Horus was eager to leave the marshes and avenge his father's death. He wanted to defeat Seth without his mother's help. So Horus went to challenge Seth at his palace. Horus said that he ought to be king in his father's place.

Seth was very polite to his nephew. He took him into the palace. He gave him food and a lot of wine to drink. He asked Horus to stay the night. Horus forgot his mother's warning. He agreed to stay with his uncle.

In the middle of the night Seth came into Horus' room and attacked him. The two gods fought. Horus punched Seth in the groin. Seth seized Horus by the head and tore out his left eye. Seth ripped the eye apart and trampled on the pieces.

The eyes of Horus had shone like the sun and the moon. When Seth put out the moon eye, the night sky went dark. The wise god Thoth collected the pieces of the lost eye. He used magic to make the damaged eye whole again. Thoth healed Horus of his wound and put the eye back in his face. So now, the Eye of Horus gives life and strength to everyone who sees it.

Thoth healed Seth as well. He told the two gods to stop fighting. Thoth said that there should be a trial, to decide who was the true king. Seth didn't like the idea, but that is what happened.

A "sacred eye" amulet in black and turquoise glaze. Eyes of this shape can be either the eye of Horus, or the eye of the sun god. Both were symbols of power. The details of the eye are probably based on the markings of a hawk. In Egyptian myth, the sky can be compared to a giant hawk whose left eye is the moon and whose right eye is the sun.

The story of how the god Thoth made the injured eye of Horus whole again may be linked to the way the moon appears to shrink and grow every month.

The "sacred eye" was one of the most common Egyptian amulets. It was thought to have healing powers and was worn for protection by the living and the dead.

"When we were little," said Thaues, "our father gave us pretty necklaces of blue beads. Some of the beads were shaped like eyes. Were they Horus eyes?"

Khonouphis nodded.

"Wearing the Eye of Horus will help to keep you safe. Do you still have the beads?"

The twins looked sad.

"We had to sell our necklaces to buy food," said Taous. "Our brother has all sorts of good things. It isn't fair."

"No," agreed Khonouphis, "but in the end there is justice, and everyone will get what they deserve."

The Revenge of Horus

Khonouphis took the twins to the main gate in the high mudbrick wall surrounding the temple.

"Long before the Greeks brought their laws to Egypt, cases were tried at temple gateways. Everyone had to swear before the god of the temple that they were telling the truth. They knew that if they lied, the god might punish them with blindness. The gods love justice, but making the right choice isn't always easy."

The trial of Horus and Seth was held at Heliopolis. The earth god, Geb, was the chief judge. All the other gods and goddesses were there. Isis spoke out. She told how she had found the murdered body of Osiris. She demanded that her son Horus should be king in his father's place. She wanted Seth punished for his crimes.

"Justice is better than force," said Shu. "Horus should be king as his father was."

Many of the gods agreed, but Seth said,

"I am the strongest of the strong. No one else can conquer the chaos monster, Apep. If Horus wants to be king, let him fight for the crown. Let him come outside with me and we'll soon see who is the stronger."

Thoth protested that Horus had a right to the crown, but some of the gods were uncertain. They felt that Seth should be king because he was older and stronger. Others thought that Seth should rule in the south of Egypt and Horus in the north. The gods needed more time to decide the case. Geb said that the court would meet again soon.

Seth was afraid that the clever words of Isis would win the gods over. He refused to appear before the court if Isis was there. The gods agreed that Horus must speak for himself. Isis was banned from the court.

The gods chose to meet next on an island in the river. They all crossed to the island in a ferryboat. The ferryman was told not to let any woman who might be Isis onto his ferry. Isis used a spell to turn herself into a bent old woman. She hobbled up to the ferryman.

"I need to take this basket of food to a young boy who is looking after cattle on the island. Please ferry me across."

The ferryman said,

"I've been warned not to let Isis get to the island, so I'm not taking any woman across."

Isis said,

"Please be kind to an old woman. I'll give you one of the cakes from my basket."

The ferryman laughed at her.

"Do you think I'd risk my job for a cake?"

Then Isis said,

"I'll give you this little gold ring from my finger, if you'll take me to the island."

The ferryman was greedy. He took the gold and ferried Isis across the river.

Once Isis was on the island, she spoke another spell. It turned her into a very beautiful young woman. Seth saw her coming. He waited under a sycamore tree and called out,

"Here, pretty one, come and spend some time with me."

Isis pretended to be very upset.

"Oh great lord, I am in such trouble. I was married to a herdsman and we had a son. We were so happy, but my husband died. My little boy wanted to look after our animals in his father's place. Then this cruel man came. He threw us out of our home and threatened to beat my son. He has taken everything we owned. If only a strong lord like you would help us ..."

Seth said,

"Of course I will. How dare this intruder treat you so badly? I will beat him with my club and throw him out of your house. Your son should have everything that belonged to his father."

Then Isis turned herself into a bird and flew up into a tree. She screeched at Seth,

"You've judged yourself out of your own mouth. You've found yourself guilty. Go beat yourself!"

Seth realized that he had been tricked by Isis. He cried tears of fury. He complained to the other gods. They laughed at him. Seth asked them to punish the ferryman for bringing Isis to the island. The gods agreed. They punished the greedy ferryman by cutting off his toes.

When Horus came to the court, many of the gods spoke in favor of giving him the crown. Seth was angrier than ever.

"If you make Horus king, I will tear the crown from his head. I will drown him in the river. Let us fight to see who should rule Egypt."

Horus did not want to look like a coward. He accepted the challenge.

Seth turned himself into a mighty hippopotamus. He plunged into the Nile. Horus and Isis got into a small boat. Isis made a magic harpoon with copper barbs. Horus used it to strike Seth in the water. He wounded him in seven different places. Then Horus dived into the river and turned himself into a hippopotamus. He fought Seth with his teeth and his tusks.

The Nile turned red with blood. Isis was afraid that Horus would be killed. She aimed at Seth with the harpoon, but she hit Horus by mistake. He screamed,

"Mother, it's me, Horus. Let go of me!"

Isis called to the magic harpoon.

"That is Horus, my son. Come out of his body."

The harpoon came back to her hand.

She threw again. This time she hit Seth. The harpoon bit deep into Seth's flesh. He screamed,

"Isis, how can you hurt me like this? You should love me. I am your brother."

For a moment, Isis felt sorry for Seth. She called to the harpoon.

"That is Seth, my brother. Come out of his body." The harpoon came back to her.

Horus was furious. Fierce as a leopard, he jumped out of the water and cut off his mother's head. The next moment Horus was horrified by what he had done, but Isis was too full of magic to be harmed easily. Thoth quickly healed her with his magic. He gave Isis the head of a cow in place of her own head. From that time on, Isis was sometimes a woman and sometimes a cow. Isis forgave Horus for cutting off her head. She knew that he had acted in the heat of battle.

Horus and Seth fought in many shapes. Seth turned himself into a red bull. Horus attacked him and cut off one of Seth's front legs. He threw it up into the sky. You can see it there still among the stars. They fought each other as lions. They fought each other as crocodiles. Seth and Horus fought each other again and again. They broke each other's bones and bit each other's flesh. They fought for eighty years, and still there was no winner.

All the other gods got tired of the fighting. The whole country was torn up by the two rivals. The gods knew that there would be no peace until the great quarrel was settled. They met again, here at Memphis. Horus and Seth came before the court. The body of Osiris was brought there too. Ra-Atum himself decided the case.

"Osiris was innocent. Seth is to blame. Horus is in the right."

A bronze amulet of Horus harpooning Seth. The hippopotamus is very small and hard to see because the Egyptians thought it was dangerous to make this evil form of Seth visible.

A harpoon is a barbed spear attached to a rope, used for killing water-dwelling animals. The Egyptians hunted hippopotami for their ivory tusks and to stop them trampling crops.

This small amulet shows how Horus won the crown of Egypt by fighting Seth. A version of the story is illustrated on the walls of the temple of Horus at Edfu.

Ra-Atum said that Horus should be made king of Egypt. He ordered that Osiris should rule the land of the dead, but he did not punish Seth.

"Seth shall live in the sky with me. He can be the god of storms, so people will always be afraid of him."

Seth was forced to agree but he was not happy. When you hear thunder over the desert, that is Seth still grumbling at his fate.

"I don't see why Seth was forgiven," complained Taous.

"When the chaos monster attacks the sun boat," answered Khonouphis, "the gods need the strength of Seth. Any family needs all its members to work together. Our own king, Ptolemy, fought a war against his brother. Now, he has forgiven his brother. They are ruling Egypt together and our country is at peace again."

The King of the Dead

Khonouphis took the twins around the outside of the great mudbrick wall.

"Look to the north, beyond the lake, and you will see one of the ancient palaces of our kings. When each new king of Egypt is to be crowned, he comes to this temple. We try to do everything just the way it was done for Horus, when he became king."

After Ra-Atum had given his judgment, Thoth brought a crown for Horus. It shone like the stars and the moon. Horus, the son of Isis, was crowned king of Egypt. He sat on the throne of his father. All the gods kissed the ground in front of him. Isis was the happiest of mothers.

Seth was forced to carry the body of Osiris to the holy city of Abydos. At last Osiris could be given a proper burial. Horus did what every son should do for his father. He followed his father's coffin to the tomb. He said prayers for Osiris.

The painted coffin of Osiris was held upright by Anubis. Horus opened the lid and touched the mummy of Osiris. He touched the nose and the mouth and the eyes and the ears.

The Egyptians copied their funeral rites from the funeral that Horus gave to Osiris.

This painting from a Book of the Dead is nearly three and a half thousand years old. It shows the funeral of a man called Hunefer. To the right is his tomb and a tomb-stone showing Hunefer with Osiris. The god Anubis holds up Hunefer's mummy, while Hunefer's wife and another woman mourn.

Behind stand two priests who are performing a magical rite to let Hunefer's spirit speak and see and hear in the afterlife. A priest wearing a leopard skin is burning incense and pouring out water. The food on the table is for Hunefer to eat in the afterlife.

He said the magic words that let the spirit of Osiris breathe and speak and see and hear again. The mummy of Osiris was put in its tomb. Osiris had been given new life, but he could not stay with his family. He belonged in the underworld now.

Horus took his father's place. To show that the spirit of Osiris would live for ever, Horus set up a column. We call it the djed column. As the column was pulled upright, Osiris rose from the tomb to be king of the underworld.

He ruled the dead just as his son Horus ruled the living. All the demons of the underworld bowed down to Osiris. The throne-room of his palace was called the Hall of the Double Truth. Every night, Isis joined her beloved Osiris there. Nephthys came too, to stand behind his throne.

Khonouphis took the twins to the west gate of the temple. From there, they could see the desert hills where all the tombs lay. The road leading to the desert was guarded by sphinxes — statues with the bodies of lions and the heads of kings.

"Everyone must travel the paths of the west," said Khonouphis, "to reach the throne-room of Osiris."

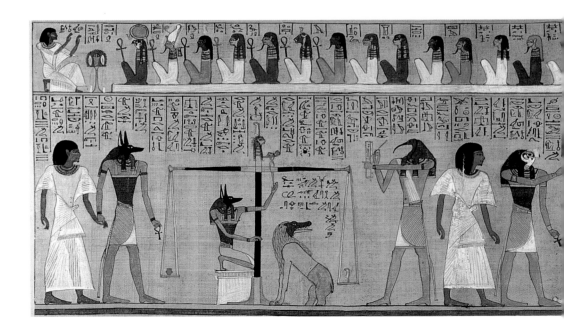

The Judgment of the Dead

Khonouphis stood looking towards the western desert and the great city of the dead. "The Apis Bull will be carried along this road to the tomb that has been made for him. All the dead should be buried in the west, where the sun sets."

The souls of the dead go down into the underworld, just as the sun god does each evening. There are many dangers in the underworld. Terrible demons try to catch souls in their nets, and huge snakes try to swallow them. Great crocodiles lurk in the rivers of the underworld, and every gateway is guarded by animal-headed demons with knives in their hands.

The souls that survive this dangerous journey are brought into the Hall of the Double Truth by Anubis. Every dead person has to stand trial in front of Osiris and the other gods of the underworld.

This picture shows what happens when the spirit of Hunefer comes before the court of Osiris in the underworld. The painting is rather like a cartoon strip as it tells several stages in the story.

To the left, Anubis leads Hunefer into the throne-room. Above, Hunefer is shown swearing to the judges of the underworld that he is innocent of any crime. The heart of Hunefer is then weighed against the feather of truth. Anyone who fails this test is eaten by the monster who squats by the scales. Hunefer is found "not guilty." The ibis-headed god, Thoth, records the verdict and Horus leads Hunefer to Osiris. Isis and Nephthys stand behind the throne of Osiris. The skin of Osiris is painted green as a symbol that he has died and come to life again, like plants which die and grow again each year. The spirit of Hunefer will now live forever as a follower of Osiris.

The dead have to swear that they didn't do harm to anyone while they were alive. Lying is no use. The wise god Thoth weighs the hearts of the dead against the feather of truth. Anyone who fails this test is thrown to a monster. She has the back legs of a hippopotamus, the front legs of a big cat, and the face of a crocodile. She bites off the heads of the bad people and gobbles up their souls.

Osiris gives everlasting life to the good people. They become shining spirits. They can live in the west with Osiris for ever. You can see Osiris in the night sky. He is there in the stars that the Greeks call Orion. Lady Isis shines as the bright star Sirius. When we see her star rising above the horizon, we know that the river Nile will rise too. Without the Nile, our country would just be empty desert.

"Will we see Father again in Osiris's country?" asked Thaues.

"If he was a good man," said Khonouphis, "he will be there to welcome you. But only the greatest of magicians can visit the kingdom of Osiris while they are still alive."

"I don't want to die and be made into a mummy," said Taous.

"Everyone has to die," answered Khonouphis. "Even the good god Osiris died. He was afraid, just as we are, but his death gave all of us hope. Speak to Osiris when you are afraid. In this temple we call him 'Osiris who listens to prayers.' "

Khonouphis pointed to another part of the desert.

"That is where we bury Osiris each year."

"But you said that he was buried in Abydos," complained Taous.

"Every temple has a tomb for Osiris. He is buried everywhere," said Khonouphis. "The black soil of the river valley is his body. Each year he lives in the crops that grow to feed his people. Each year, he is cut down again with the corn and the barley. His body is trampled and torn, but he rises each spring with the green shoots."

The twins looked at each other. They didn't understand.

"Osiris also lives and dies again in each Apis Bull," said Khonouphis. "So when we bury the bull, we are burying Osiris.

Everyone who joins in the funeral becomes part of the family of the gods. When we grieve for the bull, we are grieving like Isis and Nephthys. Now that you know their story, will you play your part as the twin goddesses?"

"We will try," promised Taous.

The Funeral of the Apis Bull

While the Apis Bull was being mummified, the twins lived with Khonouphis and his family. They were given plenty to eat and fine new clothes. Khonouphis taught the twins everything they had to say and do and sing at the funeral.

It was Osiris who gave ordinary people hope that their souls would survive the death of their bodies.

On this tombstone a royal cook and his wife are worshipping Osiris. The cook is offering bunches of lotus flowers. His wife is praying. Egyptians usually prayed standing up, with their hands raised like this.

At the bottom you can see the cook's family bringing flowers and gifts to their dead parents. Most Egyptians believed that they would be reunited with their families after death.

Thousands of people came to watch the bull's funeral. All the royal family was there. The priests of the temple dressed up as gods. They acted out the story of Osiris and the quarrel of Horus and Seth. The priests launched a papyrus boat on the temple lake. They acted out the journey of the sun god through the underworld and the fight with the chaos monster.

The mummy of the Apis Bull was hauled along on a wheeled cart. Taous and Thaues stood beside the mummy dressed as goddesses. When they remembered the story of Isis and Osiris, they both found it easy to cry. They sang sad songs to Osiris and begged him to come back to his people. The twins were with the bull all through the journey to his tomb at Saqqara. They watched the mummy lifted into its great stone coffin and stayed in the tomb all night, watching over the Apis Bull.

The next morning, the tomb was sealed and the funeral was over. The royal family was very pleased by the way that the twins had sung and acted their parts. King Ptolemy gave orders that the girls should be rewarded. As well as the silver they had earned, Taous and Thaues were given jobs for life in the temples of Saqqara. The sisters hoped that all their troubles were at an end. Every day they thanked Isis and Osiris for their good fortune.

Note

The twins

Taous and Thaues were real people. They played goddesses at the funeral of the Apis Bull who died in 164 BC. We know about them through a series of letters written on their behalf. These letters show that the twins did not always get the wages they had been promised. They also continued to have problems with their mother and their greedy half-brother.

Egypt's rulers

The two brothers, Ptolemy Philometor and Ptolemy Euergetes, who were ruling Egypt together in 164 BC, soon went back to fighting each other. Their sister, Queen Cleopatra II, married both brothers in turn.

About Egypt

The modern word Egypt comes from the Greek name for the ancient temple of Ptah at Memphis, where the twins went. Very little is left of the temple. This area of Memphis is being studied by the Egypt Exploration Society. The tombs and temples of Saqqara are better preserved. Objects that the twins might have seen survive in museums around the world. All the pictures in this book are of objects in the British Museum, London.

Further Reading

For children

British Museum Colouring Books: Ancient Egypt, British Museum Press

P.A.Clayton, *Family Life in Ancient Egypt,* Wayland

P.A.Clayton, *The Valley of the Kings,* Wayland

N.Grant, *The Egyptians,* Simon & Schuster

G.Harris, *Ancient Egypt: A Cultural Atlas for Young People,* Facts on File

G.Harris, *Gods and Pharaohs from Egyptian Mythology,* Peter Lowe/Peter Bedrick

G. Hart, *Ancient Egypt,* Dorling Kindersley Eyewitness Books

Lise Manniche, *The Ancient Egyptians Activity Book,* British Museum Press

N.Reeves, *Into the Mummy's Tomb,* Scholastic

P.Steele, *I Wonder Why the Pyramids were Built,* Kingfisher

For adults

G.Hart, *Egyptian Myths,* British Museum Press

G.Hart, *A Dictionary of Egyptian Gods and Goddesses,* Routledge & Kegan Paul

S.Quirke, *Ancient Egyptian Religion,* British Museum Press

D.Thompson, *Memphis under the Ptolemies,* Princeton University Press

Sources of the Pictures